THE 1940s HOUSE
ACTIVITY BOOK

John Malam

First published in 2001 by Channel 4 Books,
an imprint of Macmillan Publishers Ltd
25 Eccleston Place, London SW1W 9NF,
Basingstoke and Oxford.
Associated companies throughout the world.
www.macmillan.com

ISBN 0 7522 1933 2

Designed by Jane Coney
Illustrations by Jane Cradock Watson
Colour reproduction by Speedscan.
Printed and bound in Belgium by Proost

This book accompanies the television series *The
1940s House* made by Wall To Wall Television for
Channel 4.
Series Producer: Simon Shaw

PICTURE CREDITS
All pictures © Simon Roberts/Growbag except the following.
The Hymers family: 20, 34, 35, 41. Paul Bricknell: 36, 37, 42/3.
Marguerite Patten: 38. Wall To Wall Television: 38. The Imperial
War Museum: 10, 11 (top), 12, 17, 20, 22, 26, 27, 32 (middle and
bottom), 38. Topham Picturepoint: 11 (bottom), 13, 32 (top), 38
(top), 39.

ACKNOWLEDGEMENTS
The author would like to thank the following people who have
helped during the development of this book: Simon Armitage,
Margaret Barker, Paul Bricknell, Valerie Coney, Brian Curzon,
Hilary Edwards-Malam, Naomi Hall, Lillie Moore, Hazel Sear,
Emma Tait and the staff of Cheshire County Council (Libraries and
Archives), in particular Clare Ashbee, Emma Booth, Diane Jones,
Sue Maddocks, and Anne Warden. Special thanks to the Hymers
family, especially Ben and Thomas, without whom this book would
not have been possible.

Contents

Go-carting, putting and cycling – pastimes from the 1940s that children still enjoy today.

A trip through time

If you had the chance to be a time-traveller, when and where would you go to? Would it be to Ancient Egypt to find out how they really built the pyramids? Or to Ancient Rome to see gladiators fight in the Colosseum? Maybe you'd stay in Britain and visit London in the 1600s, where you'd watch William Shakespeare's plays performed at the city's theatres. Perhaps you wouldn't go that far back in time at all. You may want to visit a time not quite so different from today, a time within the living memories of many older people in Britain. This is what two boys from Yorkshire did, and this is their story.

Meet Ben and Thomas Hymers

'We are the 1940s family,' said Ben (aged 10) and Thomas (aged 7). For these brothers from Otley, West Yorkshire, time travel was about to come true.

Thomas and Ben Hymers, with their mother Kirstie, in their 1940s school uniforms.

With their mum, Kirstie, and grandparents, Lyn and Michael, Ben and Thomas Hymers had been chosen from hundreds who had applied to live in the 1940s house. They were going to take part in a living history experiment, where everything they did for nine weeks would be done just as it was in the 1940s. What's more, it was going to be filmed for television.

The 1940s House

In order to take part in the experiment, the Hymers could not stay in their own home in Yorkshire. Instead, they moved to a house in West Wickham, Kent, which had already been restored and furnished in the way it would

Ben and Thomas say goodbye to the twenty-first century.

6 APRIL 1939
Britain, France and Poland agree to help each other if war starts.

1 MAY 1939
Compulsory military service begins for men aged twenty and over.

3 MAY 1939
Campaign to encourage farmers to grow food on pasture land.

1 JULY 1939
Women's Land Army (WLA) formed.

Wearing wartime clothes and his identification tag, Thomas is ready to step back in time.

I liked playing football with Ben, building the Anderson shelter and planting seeds in the vegetable garden. Thomas

wartime became used to the sight and sound of war planes, the screech of air-raid sirens, and the panic of taking cover in air-raid shelters. They were also in what became known as 'Doodlebug Alley', the flight path which Germany's V1 flying bombs took as they raced towards the capital.

It was these vital, exciting ingredients that made West Wickham a good location for the 1940s house. But one thing needs to be said from the beginning – the Second World War affected the whole of Britain. While London may have suffered the worst of the bombing, we must remember that from Orkney and Shetland in the north (where the first German raid was made), to the Channel Islands in the south (which were occupied by German forces), every man, woman and child in the land was affected by the events of those six fateful years.

have been in the 1940s. This would be where they would live.

Situated on the southern edge of London, West Wickham made the perfect location to find out what life in 1940s Britain was really like. The time they were going to travel back to was not the London of 1948, when the capital played host to the Olympic Games, but to six of the most important years of the twentieth century. The Hymers were going to find out about life in Britain during the Second World War, 1939 to 1945.

West Wickham was chosen because of its closeness to London. The people who lived there in the

I liked playing football, being closer to the family, building the Anderson shelter, and the food – when we got some! Ben

Ben Hymers on his way to the Biggin Hill airshow. Ben and Thomas enjoyed the day, although you wouldn't guess if from the expression on Ben's face!

2 JULY 1939
Women's Auxiliary Air Force (WAAF) formed.

31 AUGUST 1939
The Royal Navy gets ready for war.

1 SEPTEMBER 1939
Operation Pied Piper begins. Children are evacuated from towns and cities.

1 SEPTEMBER 1939
Treasures are taken from London's museums to places of safety.

I didn't like going into the Anderson shelter in the middle of the night. Thomas

The adventure begins

Sunday, 16 April 2000 is a day that Ben and Thomas will remember for a long time to come. Dressed in 1940s clothes, they entered 17 Braemar Gardens, West Wickham. As soon as they walked into the house, they left the twenty-first century behind. They were about to begin living in the past.

As they entered the cosy semi-detached house, it really was like stepping back in time. Everything was old – more than fifty years old. But their new home wasn't a museum – it was real, and everything in it was for them to use. In the front room they found a large, old radio. Switching it on, it crackled into life and the voice of the Prime Minister in 1939, Neville Chamberlain, came through loud and clear. 'This country is at war…' they heard. From that

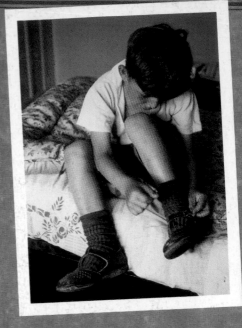

If only they had Velcro shoe fasteners in the 1940s!

moment onwards, Ben, Thomas and the rest of the Hymers family knew exactly at what point in time their adventure was to begin. Neville Chamberlain's famous speech announcing that Britain was at war with Germany was made on Sunday, 3 September 1939.

For the next nine weeks, the Hymers family went through an incredible voyage of discovery, which Ben and Thomas enjoyed from start to finish.

Toothpaste didn't come in tubes in the 1940s, as Ben and Thomas discovered.

I didn't like getting my tea late, or the National Loaf. Ben

1 SEPTEMBER 1939
The blackout begins.

1 SEPTEMBER 1939
Germany and Russia invade Poland.

3 SEPTEMBER 1939
Britain and France declare war on Germany.

3 SEPTEMBER 1939
British troops land in France.

Wherever they went, the family
wore their 1940s clothes.

The food

Ben and Thomas had to forget about burgers, pizza, fish fingers and fizzy drinks. All that convenience, pre-packed food wasn't available in 1940s Britain. And neither were a lot of other foods. The problem was that almost as soon as the war began, some foods stopped coming into the country because the ships that brought them were attacked and sunk. Fresh fruit, such as bananas from the Caribbean, were rarely seen in Britain during the war years.

To be true to life, Ben and Thomas ate the type of food that wartime children ate. Each day their mother and grandmother shopped for food at the local grocery shop (supermarkets didn't exist in the 1940s), exchanging it for coupons from the family's ration books as well as having to pay for it with the old money that you can find out about on pages 42 and 43. Meals were freshly prepared each day, but because of food shortages, often it was just not possible to follow recipes straight out of cookery books especially if some of the ingredients could not be bought because of the war.

Ben and Thomas soon found out about making meals with the limited ingredients available, with the help of the government's advice leaflets. Some they liked, some they didn't. You can try out some wartime recipes for yourself, on pages 18 and 19.

Ben dances with his mother, Kirstie, at a
dance to celebrate the end of their stay in
the 1940s. When the war ended there were
parties all over Britain.

4 SEPTEMBER 1939
Winston Churchill is
appointed First Lord
of the Admiralty.

5 SEPTEMBER 1939
USA says it will not get
involved in the war.

6 SEPTEMBER 1939
South Africa declares
war on Germany.

10 SEPTEMBER 1939
Canada declares war
on Germany.

It was scary when the air-raid siren went off. Ben

As Thomas learned, sandbags were seen in streets all over Britain during the Second World War. They were to protect buildings from bomb blasts. These are piled outside the local church hall, which Ben and Thomas visited to attend a Beetle drive. You can learn more about the Beetle game on page 41.

The air-raid siren

Another feature of wartime life was the air-raid siren. During the war, sirens were fitted to buildings across the land. At the first sign of enemy planes approaching, the wailing sound of the siren would fill the air, and people would head for cover – to refuge rooms inside their homes (cellars and basements), to small Anderson shelters in their own gardens or to larger community shelters in public places.

The war brought families closer together, as Ben and Thomas discovered.

A siren was fitted to 17 Braemar Gardens, in the hallway of the house. Just as in the war, they never knew when it was going to go off. As Ben and Thomas discovered, it was most likely to be when they were tucked up in bed, fast asleep. And when that happened, there was no time to waste. Up they got and, with the rest of the family, headed to the safety of their garden shelter.

The Anderson shelter

When the Anderson shelter arrived, it looked for all the world like pieces from a gigantic construction kit, which is just what it was. A few flat pieces of iron, a few bent pieces and a box of bolts to fix it all together.

As their grandfather dug a big hole in the garden, with some help from the neighbours (just as in the war, everyone helped each other), Ben and Thomas

I was cross when the siren went off because I had to get up in the middle of the night. Thomas

16 SEPTEMBER 1939
Petrol rationing begins.

29 SEPTEMBER 1939
National Registration Day. Everyone registers for ration books and identification cards.

30 SEPTEMBER 1939
Leaflets sent out telling people not to waste food.

1 OCTOBER 1939
250,000 men are called up for military service.

I would like to have a 1940s football because it was an ideal weight. Ben

watched – then joined in. Soon, they had their very own den – only this was not a playhouse. This was the place to be should West Wickham come under attack from enemy bombers. Of course, this was one thing that couldn't happen in the 1940s house – no one was actually going to drop bombs on them. But in the real 1940s, Braemar Gardens *had* been bombed and two houses opposite number 17 were damaged. Ben and Thomas saw a photo taken at the time.

When Ben and Thomas returned from a day at school, they were able to tell their grandmother everything they had done that day.

Time to go home

After their nine weeks in the 1940s house, it was time for Ben and Thomas to return to the present day, and their life at home in Otley. They had seen and done things that no other children today in Britain have done. As their mother, Kirstie, says: 'It's been a vital experience for them and it is something that will stay with them for the rest of their lives. I think that they have been very privileged to have been able to do this.'

Sweets were in short supply – Ben makes one last as long as he can.

I would like to have a 1940s toy Spitfire, my sword and my shield. Thomas

About this book

This book gives some answers to the question: What was it like being a child in Britain in the Second World War? It is both an information book and an activity book, looking at many of the things Ben and Thomas found out about at first hand. The wide range of activities, including quizzes, games and things to make will help you to step back into the 1940s, just as Ben and Thomas did. We hope you enjoy it!

3 OCTOBER 1939
The government starts to censor the news.

3 OCTOBER 1939
Germany tests the A4 rocket, the forerunner of the V2 rocket.

9 OCTOBER 1939
An Act of Parliament stops people charging too much for food.

13 NOVEMBER 1939
First German bombs dropped on Britain, on the Shetland Islands.

Forties flashback

What do you know about life in Britain in the 1940s? When Ben and Thomas lived in the 1940s house, they found many things were different from today.

For some people in Britain now the 1940s is not that long ago. Those people might have been children then, just like you are today. Try this quiz – it will help you to imagine what it was like in the 1940s.

GEORGE THE WHAT?

Did you know that Britain has had six kings called George? One George couldn't speak English, one was nicknamed Farmer George, and one was king during the 1940s.

1: Who was king in the 1940s?

a) George III

b) George IV

c) George VI

A GREAT LEADER

For most of the Second World War, Britain's government was led by a great Prime Minister. He was much liked by the people.

2: Who was Prime Minister for most of the Second World War?

a) Benjamin Disraeli

b) Tony Blair

c) Winston Churchill

This man was Britain's wartime Prime Minister.

OCCUPIED BY GERMANY

In 1940, German soldiers took control of a group of British islands. They were the only part of Britain occupied during the Second World War.

4: Which British islands did Germany occupy?

a) The Channel Islands

b) The Orkney Islands

c) The Scilly Isles

KNOW YOUR DATES

The Second World War was the last major international war. It lasted six years, and it affected everyone in Britain.

3: During which years did the Second World War take place?

a) 1913 to 1919

b) 1939 to 1945

c) 1950 to 1956

We thought the 1940s seemed like a very long time ago.
Ben and Thomas

20 NOVEMBER 1939
Germans use mines against British ships in the North Sea.

4 DECEMBER 1939
King George VI visits British troops in France.

10 DECEMBER 1939
Nobel Prizes are awarded. There is no Nobel Peace Prize this year.

19 DECEMBER 1939
Canadian troops arrive in Britain.

SPORT FOR ALL
The Olympic Games were not held in 1940 or 1944. They began again after the Second World War, in 1948.

5: Which was the host city of the 1948 Olympic Games?

a) Berlin

b) Paris

c) London

FUNNY MONEY
In the 1940s, 12 pennies made 1 shilling, and there were 20 shillings in £1.

6: In the 1940s, how many pennies were in £1?

a) 220

b) 240

c) 260

This man led Germany in the Second World War. Do you know who he was?

IT'S IN THE CAN
Food was in short supply during the Second World War. To make up for a shortage of fresh meat, the USA sent tinned meat to Great Britain.

7: What was the American tinned meat called?

a) Wham

b) Spam

c) Clam

FLYING HIGH AND FAST
Towards the end of the Second World War a new type of plane was seen in our skies. Today, they are everywhere. You might even have flown in one.

8: What was the new type of plane?

a) Microlight plane

b) Rocket plane

c) Jet plane

PUBLIC ENEMY NO. 1
Germany's wartime leader was the most hated man in Britain. He wanted to invade Britain but luckily for us he never did.

9: Who was Germany's leader during the Second World War?

a) Martin Hitler

b) Rudolf Hitler

c) Adolf Hitler

The king visits people who have lost their homes.

I HEARD IT ON THE RADIO
In the 1940s, people listened to the radio far more than they do today. There were radio programmes just for children.

10: What was the name of a popular children's radio show?

a) Children's House

b) Children's Hello

c) Children's Holiday

How well do you think you've done? Turn to page 46 to check your answers. Will you be a wartime wizard or not?

1 JANUARY 1940
Two million men aged nineteen to twenty-seven are called up for military service.

8 JANUARY 1940
'Coupon Monday': food rationing begins for butter, bacon, sugar and meat.

24 JANUARY 1940
The 'Derby' horse race is cancelled.

27 JANUARY 1940
Britain is hit by storms, the worst in living memory.

Get out of town

For tens of thousands of British children, Friday 1 September 1939 was a day to remember. As dawn broke, Operation Pied Piper began. In towns and cities across the country, children set off to school where they gathered in their playgrounds. They took with them the few belongings they were allowed – the government had issued separate lists for boys and girls. At school they were put into groups and taken to their local railway stations. They were sent to live in safety with families in the countryside. These children were called 'evacuees'.

Evacuees' essentials

This is what the government told school children to take on their journey:

Evacuees on their way to their temporary homes.

BOYS
2 vests
2 pairs of underpants
2 shirts
2 nightshirts or pairs of pyjamas
2 pairs of socks
2 pairs of boots or shoes
1 pair of Wellingtons (if possible)
1 warm coat and/or mackintosh
1 pair of trousers
1 pullover
6 handkerchiefs
1 toothbrush
1 face flannel
1 comb
2 towels

GIRLS
2 vests
2 liberty bodices (if worn)
2 pairs of knickers
2 nightdresses or pairs of pyjamas
2 pairs of socks or stockings
2 pairs of shoes
1 pair of Wellingtons (if possible)
1 warm coat and/or mackintosh
1 warm dress or tunic and jersey
1 cardigan
2 cotton frocks
6 handkerchiefs
1 toothbrush
1 face flannel
1 comb
2 towels

BOYS AND GIRLS
gas mask
identity card
ration book
clothing and personal coupons
food for one day

We think evacuees would have been scared and sad at having to leave their families behind.
Ben and Thomas

6 FEBRUARY 1940
Public told that: 'Careless talk costs lives' and 'Be like Dad keep Mum'.

26 FEBRUARY 1940
300 British prisoners-of-war are rescued from a German tanker.

28 FEBRUARY 1940
The *Queen Elizabeth* sails to America where she stays until the war ends.

2 MARCH 1940
Oxford and Cambridge Boat Race is cancelled.

For many children life in the country was an exciting new adventure.

■ EVACUATION
▨ NEUTRAL
▦ SAFE

Safe areas

This map shows you where children were evacuated from and where they were sent to. Children were evacuated from those towns and cities that were most likely to be attacked to quieter, safer parts of the country like the children pictured here. Some places were 'neutral' which meant children were not evacuated from these areas and no children were evacuated to them either. Where do you live? Do you think you would have been an evacuee?

Make an identification label

On their journeys, the evacuees had to wear identification labels fixed to their clothes. The labels said who they were and where they came from. Here's how to make one of your own.

You will need:
thin white card
scissors
ruler
20cm piece of string
felt-tip pen

1 Draw the label outline on to the card. Follow the measurements shown here. Cut it out. Cut the corners off at one end of the label. At this end, carefully make a small hole through the label.

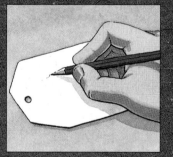

2 Write clearly on your label the name of your education authority (ask your teacher or your parents), your last name followed by your first name and your school and town.

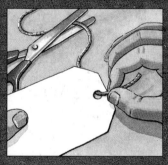

3 Thread the string through the hole in your label. Attach the label to your clothes by tying it through a buttonhole.

11 MARCH 1940
Meat rationing begins.

15 MARCH 1940
The wartime ban on football matches is lifted.

16 MARCH 1940
German air raids claim their first British civilian fatality, at the Scapa Flow naval base, Orkney.

19 MARCH 1940
A woman is fined £75 for buying 140 weeks' sugar ration in one go.

13

Air raids and shelters

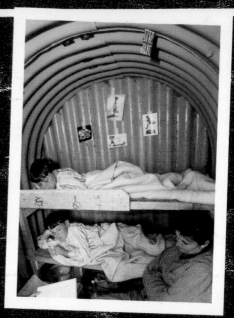

The greatest danger for the people of Britain came from the skies. Enemy planes flew on bombing missions to the country's towns and cities, especially those which had factories where goods for the war were made. Their main mission was to destroy British industry. But the bombs did not always hit these targets and many fell on people's houses. Even before the war began, the government had made plans for the protection of the population. A simple metal shelter was designed, called the Anderson shelter. The Hymers spent many nights in their Anderson shelter. It was cramped and damp, as they quickly discovered.

Other shelters

Anderson shelters were not the only places where people went for safety when they heard the siren. In London, eighty underground stations provided nightly shelter for thousands of people. The capital was the home of the biggest air-raid shelter, which had room for 11,000 people. Communal shelters were built in many other towns and cities too. People even sheltered in caves and old mine workings.

The Hymers spent a lot of time in their Anderson shelter, and even had to sleep in it overnight sometimes.

Anderson shelter floor plan

This floor plan shows how the furniture inside an Anderson shelter might be arranged, but families were free to arrange things the way they liked.

◄——————— 6ft 6in (198cm) ———————►

CUPBOARD	BED/BUNK 1
ENTRANCE	TABLE
BOOKCASE	BED/BUNK 2

The Anderson shelter was cold and there was a leak in the roof which made it damp inside. Thomas

10 MAY 1940
Winston Churchill becomes Prime Minister.

14 MAY 1940
Local Defence Volunteers (LDV) formed.

22 MAY 1940
Government takes control over most aspects of British life.

27 MAY 1940
Germans capture Boulogne in northern France, cutting off British troops.

Run for the shelter

When the air-raid siren sounded, often in the middle of the night, people rushed from their house, into the garden and the safety of their Anderson shelter. Time yourself to find out how quickly you can reach the Anderson shelter in this maze. Can you do it in less than two minutes?

START

FINISH

FACTBOX

About the Anderson shelter

It was named after Sir John Anderson, the politician in charge of people's safety.

It was free to families who earned less than £250 per year. Families who earned more than this had to pay £7.

It was made from six curved steel panels for the roof and sides and five flat pieces for the ends. It was held together with bolts.

It stood in a hole in the ground and soil was piled on the roof for protection.

30 MAY 1940
The first British

4 JUNE 1940
A total of 338,226

4 JUNE 1940
Winston Churchill

10 JUNE 1940
Italy declares war

Rationing

When war broke out, ships bringing food to Britain came under attack. Soon, food was in short supply and so the government had to act to stop people from panicking. Towards the end of 1939 everyone was given a ration book. This was a small booklet filled with coupons for different items of food.

On 8 January 1940, food rationing came into force and from then on the ration books were used. Everyone was allowed a certain amount of food per week. You could only buy food if you had enough coupons in your ration book. Each time you bought something, the shopkeeper cut out or crossed out the coupons in your book. He did this to stop people from buying more than they were entitled to.

Weekly food ration for one adult

Rations varied throughout the war years, depending on what food and how much was available. Some weeks the quantities available were less than those shown in this basic list:

Bacon and ham: 4oz (100g)

Meat: 1 shilling 2 pence worth (about £2 in today's money)

Butter: 2oz (50g)

Cheese: 2oz (50g)

Margarine: 4oz (100g)

Cooking fat: 4oz (100g)

Milk: 3 pints (1800ml)

Tea: 2oz (50g)

Sugar: 8oz (225g)

Eggs: 1

Ration coupons were used to buy food and clothes. At the top of the page Ben and Thomas's mother and grandmother work out what they can afford with their ration coupons. The Hymers used their food coupons at the local grocer's shop.

THESE ITEMS WERE ALSO AVAILABLE:

Dried milk: 1 packet every 4 weeks

Dried eggs: 1 packet every 4 weeks

Sweets: 12oz (350g) every 4 weeks

Preserves (jams): 1lb (450g) every 8 weeks

Mr Lovegrove the grocer weighing the Hymers' food.

20 JUNE 1940
Australian and New Zealand troops arrive in Britain.

24 JUNE 1940
Britain's biggest air-raid shelter is opened in London, for 11,000 people.

25 JUNE 1940
German troops given English phrase books in readiness for the invasion of Britain.

1 JULY 1940
Germany invades the Channel Islands.

A little goes a long way

At the start of rationing in January 1940, an adult was allowed 4oz (100g) of butter per week. By the middle of the war the butter ration for an adult had been reduced to 2oz (50g) per week. How far do you think 2oz (50g) of butter could be made to go? Try this, and you'll find out.

1 Cut some bread into slices, 12cm long and 8cm wide (this is about the size of bread in the 1940s).

2 Weigh out 2oz (50g) of butter (or margarine if you prefer).

3 Pat the butter or margarine into a small block.

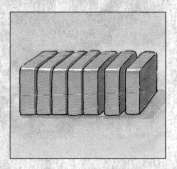

4 Divide the block into seven equal parts (one for each day of the week).

5 Take one part and spread it thinly onto your slices of bread.

How many slices of bread did your day's butter ration cover? If you were very careful, you may have been able to spread it over four, or even five, pieces.

This 1940s photograph shows women queueing to buy food. This was not an unusual sight during the Second World War.

I didn't like the idea of not being able to eat what I wanted. Ben

10 JULY 1940 German air force bombs British ships in the English Channel.

10 JULY 1940 First large-scale bombing of Britain, on docks in south Wales.

10 JULY 1940 The Battle of Britain begins.

11 JULY 1940 People asked to give aluminium pots and pans, to be made into aircraft parts

Ration book recipes

Many kinds of food were in short supply. This meant that people had to think of new ways of cooking what food was available. The government's new department, the Ministry of Food, issued leaflets with ideas for recipes. One leaflet, called *How to Use Stale Crusts*, gave ideas for how to use up left-over bread. This was just as well, because a government official had said it was illegal to feed bread to birds. The government used two cartoon characters, Doctor Carrot and Potato Pete to tell people, especially children, about the goodness in food.

Welsh rarebit

Serves 4

40g stale bread crusts
4 tablespoons milk
50g grated cheese
1 teaspoon mustard
1 teaspoon salt
pinch of pepper
15g margarine
4 rounds of toast

1 Soak the stale crusts in water. Squeeze them out. Put the soaked crusts into a bowl. Add the milk, half the cheese, the salt, pepper and mustard. Stir until well mixed.

2 Ask an adult to melt the margarine in a saucepan, then add the bread-and-cheese mixture. Stir well. Cook until hot.

3 Spread the mixture on to the rounds of toast. Sprinkle the rest of the cheese over the toast. Grill until the topping is light brown. Serve hot.

During the years of rationing the government sent out leaflets, telling people how to make the most of the food they had.

Famous food

One of the most famous of all wartime recipes was Lord Woolton's Pie. It was named after Frederick Woolton, the Minister of Food, and was created by a chef at the Savoy Hotel in London. It was a pie without any meat. Potatoes, cauliflowers, carrots, swedes, parsnips and onions all went into the pie. It was served with gravy – and more vegetables!

23 JULY 1940
The Local Defence Volunteers are given a new name the Home Guard.

15 AUGUST 1940
Heaviest air battles of the Battle of Britain.

17 AUGUST 1940
Hitler declares blockade of British Isles.

18 AUGUST 1940
The first German plane is brought down over Britain.

Crunchies

Makes 20 crunchies
100g margarine, lard
or dripping
50g sugar
50g golden syrup
125g plain flour
100g medium oatmeal
1 teaspoon baking
powder
vanilla flavouring

1 Put the fat, sugar and syrup into a large mixing bowl. Mix until smooth. Add the flour, oatmeal, baking powder and a few drops of vanilla flavouring. Stir well, until the mixture has become a stiff dough.

2 Sprinkle some flour on to a work surface. Put the dough on the work surface. With a rolling pin roll out the dough until it is about 1cm thick all over.

3 Cut the dough into pieces about 8cm long and 4cm wide. Lightly grease a baking tray. Place them on the tray. Bake at 180°C/350°F/Gas 4 for about 20 minutes or until they are golden brown.

TIP To keep your crunchies fresh, store them in an air-tight tin.

FACTBOX

Fake Food

Wartime cooks dreamt up some amazing recipes. Here are three tasty-sounding dishes and what they actually contained.

MOCK CRAB
margarine, egg and cheese.

MOCK BANANA
parsnips, milk and banana flavouring.

MOCK APRICOT TART
grated carrot, plum jam and almond flavouring.

Rhyme time

Doctor Carrot was described as 'the children's best friend', while Potato Pete had his own rhyme:

Potato Pete, Potato Pete,
See him coming down the street,
Shouting his good things to eat,
'Get your hot potatoes
from Potato Pete.'

I liked sausages, and treacle sponge and custard the best. I didn't like lumpy mashed potatoes and gravy. Ben

23 AUGUST 1940
First bombs fall
on central London.

26 AUGUST 1940
The RAF bombs Berlin,
the German capital.

27 AUGUST 1940
Towns and cities across
Britain bombed in
night-time air raids.

7 SEPTEMBER 1940
The blitz on London
begins

Lights out in the blackout!

Imagine you're an enemy pilot on a mission to bomb Britain in the Second World War. A town with all its lights switched on would be an easy target to see – but not if the lights were off.

During the war, families covered the doors and windows of their homes with curtains, sheets or thick paper. Then they covered the edges with sticky tape. Minimal light was permitted outside too. They did this every night to stop light being seen by enemy aircraft. This was known as the 'blackout'. To pass the time, families played games during the blackout. Ben and Thomas played card games and Ludo (a board game with counters). Some games such as Newmarket were played with ordinary playing cards, but Tell-tale Tracks had its own special cards, as you can see here.

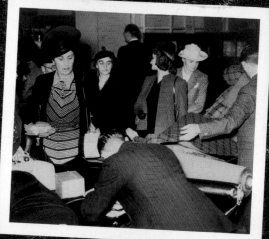

There was a rush for blackout material in shops.

Tell-tale Tracks

Here are three of the cards from Tell-tale Tracks. Can you guess what – or who – made the tracks?

In the blackout we played games and we went to bed. Ben and Thomas

One of the first jobs the Hymers had to do was to make the blackout for all the windows.

15 SEPTEMBER 1940
London, Southampton, Bristol, Cardiff, Liverpool and Manchester bombed.

15 SEPTEMBER 1940
185 German planes shot down over London.

10 OCTOBER 1940
A bomb lands on St Paul's Cathedral, London.

13 OCTOBER 1940
Princess Elizabeth, aged fourteen, makes her first radio broadcast, to evacuees.

What do you think they are? Turn to page 46 to check your answers.

F

G

E

D

Ben and Thomas play cards while their grandfather reads a magazine.

Darken your house at night

Even before the war began, the government printed booklets telling people how to darken their homes at night. One booklet, called *The Protection of Your Home Against Air Raids*, informed people that:

- Curtains must be dark and thick.
- Windows must be covered with dark blankets, carpets or thick sheets of paper.
- Outside lights, garden and porch lights must not be used. (If they are electric, the bulbs must be removed.)

People could follow the war by listening to the radio and looking for the places on a map, as Thomas is doing here.

IDEA

Why not draw up your own mystery tracks, using present-day things such as mini-scooters, skateboards, and rollerblades?

31 OCTOBER 1940
The Battle of Britain ends.

14 NOVEMBER 1940
Coventry is devastated by German bombing.

3 DECEMBER 1940
Extra Christmas rations of tea and sugar are allowed.

12 DECEMBER 1940
Sheffield bombed.

Dig for victory

Before the Second World War, much of Britain's food came from overseas. Nearly all of this food came by ship. Almost as soon as the war started, Britain's cargo ships were attacked and sunk, so that a lot of food was lost. In 1940, the government took steps to save the people of Britain from starving. First, they introduced rationing. Later in the year they began an advertising campaign called 'Dig for Victory' which encouraged people to grow their own food.

Here you can see the vegetable garden at the 1940s house. The Hymers family grew carrots, onions and peas here.

FACTBOX

Finding food

By 1943, there were 3.5 million allotments in Britain, producing more than 1 million tonnes of vegetables a year.

Farmers turned an area of pasture the size of Wales into arable (food-growing) land.

Some people kept rabbits and chickens in their gardens for meat and eggs.

Places to grow food

Up and down the country, farmers ploughed up their pastures (grass land). They planted staple foods, such as wheat and potatoes. But it wasn't only farmers who dug for victory. In towns, parks, school fields and other open spaces were made into allotments, where people could grow fruit and vegetables. Many people dug up their lawns and flower beds. Even a small garden could produce enough food – such as potatoes, tomatoes, apples, pears and plums – to feed a family. These pictures show two unusual places where food was really grown during the war – in Hyde Park, London, near the famous Albert Memorial built by Queen Victoria, and on the roof of an Anderson shelter!

2 JANUARY 1941
German planes bomb Ireland, despite the country not being in the war.

12 FEBRUARY 1941
The first patient is successfully treated with penicillin.

17 MARCH 1941
Women are urged to volunteer for jobs in factories.

9 APRIL 1941
Birmingham bombed.

Growing cress

You will need
packet of cress seeds
small tray with sides
about 3cm high
kitchen paper

1 Fold two or three sheets of kitchen paper and place in the bottom of the tray. Sprinkle water onto the paper until it is damp, but not soaking.

TIP Start a second tray a few days after the first. By the time you have harvested the cress in the first tray, the cress in the second tray will be ready to pick.

2 Scatter cress seeds on to the damp paper. Don't scatter them too thickly. Don't use all the seeds, save some to use later. Cover the tray with a sheet of clean, dry kitchen paper. Put the tray on a windowsill, where there is plenty of light for the seeds.

3 Check the seeds every day and keep the paper moist. When the seedlings are 2½cm high, take the paper cover away. When the stems are about 5cm high, the cress is ready to cut and eat.

War song
People sang songs about the Dig for Victory campaign. Here are the words of one of them:

Dig! Dig! Dig! And your muscles will grow big,
Keep on pushing the spade!
Don't mind the worms,
Just ignore the squirms,
And when your back aches laugh with glee,
And keep on diggin',
Till we give our foes a wiggin',
Dig! Dig! Dig! to victory.

HOW TO DIG

A GUIDE TO GROWING AND COOKING—

The GARDEN FRONT

GARDEN HINTS

JANUARY TO FEBRUARY ISSUE

Leaflets told people how to grow their own food.

1 MAY 1941
Liverpool bombed.

11 MAY 1941
London heavily bombed – Houses of Parliament, Westminster Abbey and Buckingham Palace damaged.

15 MAY 1941
Flight of Britain's first jet fighter, the Gloster E28/39.

2 JUNE 1941
Ration coupons are introduced for clothing.

Flying bombs

Towards the end of the Second World War, south-east Britain came under attack from Germany's 'secret weapon'– the V1, a pilotless petrol-driven plane loaded with 850kg (1,870lb) of explosives. As it reached its target, it ran out of petrol and fell out of the sky. People called these flying bombs 'doodlebugs' or 'buzz-bombs'. About 8,000 were fired at Britain and about 2,000 landed on London. The area where the 1940s house stood was known as 'Doodlebug Alley'.

Ben and Thomas's grandmother listening to the sounds of the doodlebugs.

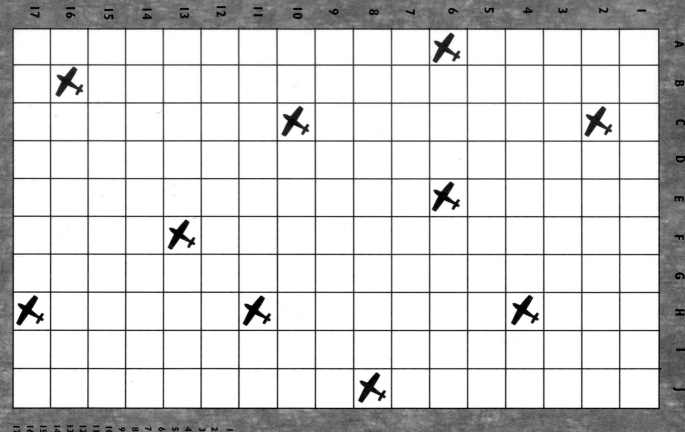

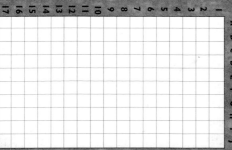

20 JUNE 1941
RADAR declared crucial in detecting German bombers.

4 JULY 1941
Coal rationing begins.

2 DECEMBER 1941
Unmarried women between 20 and 30 are called up for military service.

8 DECEMBER 1941
USA declares war on Germany, Italy and Japan.

Doodlebug game for two players

Turn this book sideways and sit opposite each other with the book between you. Hold a piece of card down the centre of the book, so you can't see your opponent's page. On each grid there are silhouettes of ten doodlebugs, flying towards London. You are a fighter pilot. You have tried shooting them down but you have run out of ammunition. The only way you can destroy them is by nudging them off course with your wing-tips. Take turns to call out co-ordinates for the squares (for example C3, F9, and so on). Each time you call out a square on your opponent's grid, mark it off on your small grid (in pencil so you can rub it out and play again). This way you won't call the same square twice. Your opponent must say whether you've scored a hit or a miss. The first one to find and destroy all ten doodlebugs is the winner.

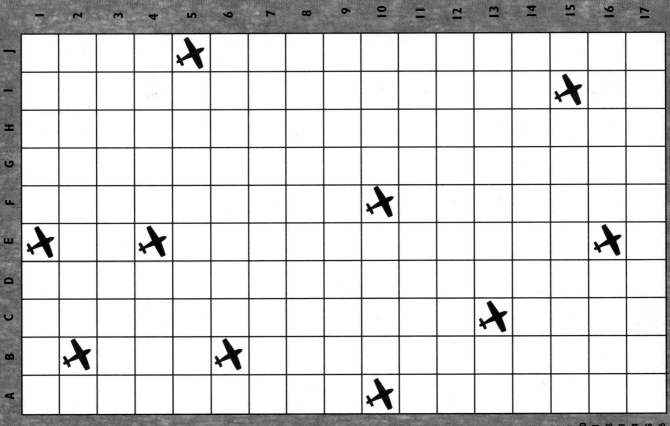

IDEA

Play the game again by adding extra doodlebugs on the grids. Remember to use pencil, so you can rub them out and play again using different squares.

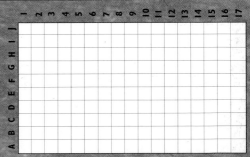

8 DECEMBER 1941
Britain declares war on Japan, Finland, Romania and Hungary.

15 DECEMBER 1941
The government says more scrap metal must be collected.

25 DECEMBER 1941
British surrender Hong Kong to the Japanese

18 FEBRUARY 1942
People urged to take fewer baths in less water and to share bath water.

Plane spotting

In the summer and autumn of 1940, air-raid sirens sounded as German planes flew in to drop their bombs on towns and cities in Britain. It was the start of the 'blitz'. The skies were not only filled with enemy aircraft. Planes of the Royal Air Force (RAF) and, later in the war, the United States Army Air Force (USAAF), crossed the English Channel on bombing missions to Germany. With so many different planes to see, British children found a new hobby. They became plane spotters and children like Ben and Thomas kept notebooks recording all the planes they had seen. To help them identify the planes, they used guidebooks which showed aircraft as black silhouettes like the ones you can see opposite.

The blitz

For people in London, Saturday, 7 September 1940, was a night to remember. That was the night planes of the German Luftwaffe (air force) began regularly bombing the city. The 'blitz' had begun, and it lasted until May 1941. It was named after the German word *blitzkrieg*, meaning 'lightning war'. It was a time of almost daily air raids. The German plan was to bomb London and other British towns and cities, forcing the country to surrender.

Thomas found out what it was like to sit at the controls of a wartime Spitfire when the whole family went to the Biggin Hill airshow.

The Battle of Britain

The air war fought by Britain and Germany over the south-east of Britain, from 10 July to 31 October 1940, became known as the Battle of Britain. The German plan was to destroy the RAF, leaving the way clear for an invasion by land. The Germans lost the battle – 2,838 of their planes were shot down. The RAF lost 1,446. Britain was never invaded.

It would have been scary to live through an air raid. You would never have known if you were going to get hit. Ben

3 MARCH 1942
Utility clothing introduced to save cloth. Shorter skirts for women, no turn-ups for men.

22 MARCH 1942
First Morse Code message sent by the BBC to the French Resistance Movement.

15 APRIL 1942
Embroidery is banned on women's underwear.

23 APRIL 1942
German air force told to destroy British towns listed in a guide book. Exeter is hit first.

SILHOUETTES IN THE SKY

I-spy planes

Here are the silhouettes of some fighter and bomber planes and a flying bomb ('doodlebug'), from the Second World War. See if you can match the descriptions to the silhouettes. Turn to page 46 to check your answers.

1• FOCKE-WULF 190
Nationality: German
Type: Fighter
Facts: 1 engine; 1 crewman; 4 machine guns and 2 wing cannon; top speed 402mph (643km/h); range 950 miles (1,530km)

2• SPITFIRE
Nationality: British
Type: Fighter
Facts: 1 engine; 1 crewman; 8 machine guns; top speed 408mph (656km/h); range 980 miles (1,577km)

3•DORNIER 217
Nationality: German
Type: Heavy bomber
Facts: 2 engines; 4 crewmen; 5 cannon; 5,550lb (2,500kg) of bombs; top speed 330mph (528km/h); range 2,400 miles (3,840km)

4• HURRICANE
Nationality: British
Type: Fighter
Facts: 1 engine; 1 crewman; 12 machine guns; 500lb (226kg) of bombs; top speed 327mph (526km/h); range 460 miles (740km)

5• FLYING BOMB OR 'VI'
Nationality: German
Type: Pilotless aircraft
Facts: 1 engines; 0 crew; 1,870lb (850kg) of explosives; top speed 400mph (640km/h); range 150 miles (240km)

6• HEINKEL 111
Nationality: German
Type: Heavy bomber
Facts: 2 engines; 6–10 crewmen; 13 machine guns; 6,000lb (2,724kg) of bombs; top speed 295mph (472km/h); range 1,100 miles (1,750km)

7• LANCASTER
Nationality: British
Type: Heavy bomber
Facts: 4 engines; 5 crewmen; 6 cannon; 4,400lb (2,000kg) of bombs; top speed 250mph (400km/h); range 1,750 miles (2,800km)

8• JUNKERS 88
Nationality: German
Type: Day and night fighter
Facts: 2 engines; 3 crewmen; 8 cannon; top speed 300mph (480km/h); range 1,250 miles (2,000km)

9• BOEING B-17 FLYING FORTRESS
Nationality: USA
Type: Heavy bomber
Facts: 4 engines; 6–10 crewmen; 13 machine guns; 6,000lb (2,724kg) of bombs; top speed 295mph (472km/h); range 1,100 miles (1,750km)

10• MESSERSCHMITT 109
Nationality: German
Type: Fighter
Facts: 1 engine; 1 crewman; 2 machine guns and 3 cannon; 550lb (250kg) of bombs; top speed 428mph (685km/h); range 350 miles (560km)

25 APRIL 1942
Princess Elizabeth, aged sixteen, registers for war service.

26 MAY 1942
Britain and Russia join forces against Germany.

31 MAY 1942
1,000 bombers attack Cologne, Germany.

29 JUNE 1942
London received news that over one million Jews have been killed by the Germans.

The battle for fuel

Everyone was encouraged to collect and sort salvage.

In wartime Britain, when food and other essential goods were in short supply, people learned to be less wasteful. They were thankful for what little they had. People found many ways of making things last longer, and they shared what they had with neighbours and friends. Because everyone was in the same situation, there was a feeling of togetherness. The public also played an important part in the war effort. People collected scrap metal, paper and rags, all of which could be used in factories making goods for the war. In 1942, the government introduced the Fuel Saving Scheme. People were asked to use less coal and electricity in their homes. Saving these fuels meant there would be more for the factories. In the 1940s house, Ben found out at first hand what the 'Battle for Fuel' was like when he became the household fuel warden.

Bathtime

Many homes in Britain used to be fitted with coal-fired boilers. Coal was burned inside them, and the heat they produced was used to make warm water for washing and bathing. One way the government saved fuel during the Second World War was by asking people to have no more than one bath a week. The result was that less coal was burned in people's homes, and, therefore, much-needed fuel was saved for use in factories. When it was time for the weekly bath, people were asked to wash in less than 5 inches (12½cm) of water. Many families painted a line on the inside of their bath, which marked this water limit. Even King George VI had a line painted around his bath!

Ben's first duty as fuel warden was to paint a line on the bath.

BEN'S FUEL WARDEN DUTIES

Set a fuel target for the house of 50 units per week.

Checked the gas and electricity meters every day to see how many units of fuel were being used.

Painted a line inside the bath to make sure no one used more than 5 inches (12½cm) of water at bathtime.

Set a limit of three shovelfuls of coal per day.

Switched off lights when they were not needed.

Shared bath water with his brother Thomas.

27 JULY 1942
Sweet rationing introduced.

31 JULY 1942
All non-essential driving banned.

31 JULY 1942
Oxford Committee for Famine Relief (OXFAM) founded.

17 AUGUST 1942
American Flying Fortress bombers make their first raid on Germany.

Can you save fuel?

This is a project to be followed over the course of two weeks. The aim is to see if your house can can use less electricity in the second week than it did in the first. You will need some help from an adult.

WEEK 1

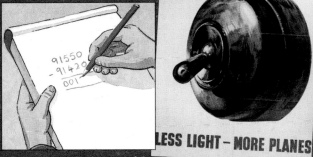

Switch off that LIGHT!

LESS LIGHT – MORE PLANES

1 Ask an adult to show you where the electricity meter for your house is kept. Write down the number shown on the meter. Ask an adult to show you which number it is.

2 After seven days, take a second reading.

3 Subtract the first number from the second number. This will show you how many units of electricity your house has used in the first week.

WEEK 2

4 For the next seven days, switch off all unnecessary electrical appliances. Make sure lights are not left on in rooms if no one is in them, switch off the TV, radio, CD player and computer if no one is using them. There will be many other things you can switch off or use less.

5 At the end of the seventh day, take another reading from the meter. Subtract from it the reading you took in step 3. This will tell you how many units of electricity your house has used in the second week. Compare the two, has your house used less fuel this week or more?

WARNING!
Ask permission from an adult before you carry out this activity. Make sure they understand what you would like to do. Always ask an adult to be with you when you are taking readings from the electricity meter.

FACTBOX

What about cars?

Petrol rationing was introduced in 1939, and after 1942 there was no petrol at all for private cars.

Some cars were converted to run on gas instead of petrol. They were not very successful.

The reason I did the fuel monitoring was because fuel was needed for ships for transporting war goods and troops to places where the army needed them to fight, and the factories needed it too. Ben

---

25 AUGUST 1942
The Duke of Kent (the King's brother) dies on active service.

3 OCTOBER 1942
British commando raid on Sark, Channel Islands.

25 OCTOBER 1942
Milk ration is reduced to 2½ pints per week.

25 OCTOBER 1942
Icing banned on cakes.

Make do and mend

It is hard for us today to imagine what it was like for the people of Britain in the Second World War. Goods that had been available before the war – such as ladies' nylon stockings – could no longer be bought and from June 1941 clothes were rationed. People learned how to live without many of the things they had before the war. Everyone had to 'make do and mend'. Instead of throwing clothes away because they were worn out, they had to be repaired or the material used to make something new. Everything had to last as long as possible, and often people thought of surprising ways of doing this.

For Ben and Thomas, living in the 1940s house meant they tried out some new things that would have helped. French knitting was a way of making odds and ends of wool go further.

Thomas watches Kirstie knitting.

French knitting

Ben and Thomas found a French knitting bobbin in the 1940s house, and they had a go at using it. You may need to buy a bobbin before you can do this activity – or make your own from a wooden cotton reel or a wine-maker's cork. The knitted wool can be coiled and sewn together to make a hat.

You will need:
French knitting bobbin
(available from
craft shops)
bodkin
4-ply (fine) wool

1 Tie a loose knot about 10cm from the end of your wool. Thread the knotted end of the wool up through the hole in the bobbin.

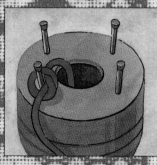

2 Slip the knot over one of the nails.

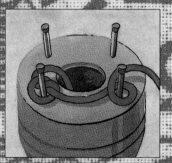

3 Working anti-clockwise, take the wool and loop it around nail 2, exactly as shown in the picture.

4 Loop the wool around nails 3 and 4, in the same way that you looped it around nail 2.

15 NOVEMBER 1942
Church bells ring for the first time since 1940 to celebrate a battle victory in North Africa.

1 DECEMBER 1942
Plans are announced for a Welfare State after the war is over.

13 DECEMBER 1942
Jews in Britain hold a day of mourning.

13 JANUARY 1943
School uniforms must only be grey or blue to save on dye.

5 Pull the end of the wool at the bottom of the bobbin to tighten the knot and take up the slack.

6 Wind the wool around the outside of all four nails, above the first ring of wool.

7 Hold the loose end of wool against the bobbin. Starting at nail 1, use the bodkin to lift the lower loop over the upper ring of wool and the nail. Repeat until you have lifted the lower loops over all four nails.

8 Pull the loose end of wool at the bottom of the bobbin to tighten your work.

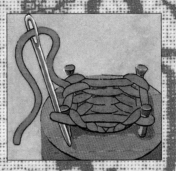

9 Wrap another ring of wool around the nails. Repeat steps 7 and 8. Carry on doing this, and eventually you will see the knitted wool appear at the bottom of the bobbin.

10 To start knitting in another colour, cut the wool away from the nails. Join a new colour, then carry on as before.

11 When your knitting is the length you want, it's time to cast it off from the bobbin. To do this, cut the wool a few centimetres away from the nails. Use the bodkin to thread the end through the loop on the nails. Lift the wool off the bodkin each time you have threaded it through the loop. Pull the knitting through the bottom of the bobbin.

When Ben and Thomas's socks wore out, Kirstie had to darn the holes so that they could keep wearing them.

FACTBOX

Clever ideas

Women who didn't have nylon stockings found a way of making it look like they did. They put cold tea or gravy browning on their legs. When it was dry it looked like brown stockings. Then they drew thin lines down the back of their legs for the stocking seams!

Offcuts of white nylon, which was used to make parachutes, were used to make underwear – and dusters could be made into dresses!

3 MARCH 1943
The King works part-time in a munitions factory.

7 MARCH 1943
The 'Wings for Victory' savings scheme begins.

16–20 MARCH 1943
German submarines sink twenty-one British merchant ships in the Atlantic.

20 APRIL 1943
Church bells can be rung again on a regular basis.

Gas masks

Hitler will send no warning – so always carry your gas mask

ISSUED BY THE MINISTRY OF HOME SECURITY

Britain had started to prepare for war even before fighting began. The government wondered what weapons were going to be used against the British people. In particular, they were worried that poison gas might be used. If bombs filled with deadly gas were dropped on to towns and cities, thousands would die if they breathed it in. To protect the population, the government issued gas masks for people to wear if there was a gas attack. The masks were made to filter out poison in the air, letting people breathe clean air. People had to carry their gas masks wherever they went. They carried them in cardboard boxes.

Make your own gas mask

You will need:
thin white card
(two sheets of A4)
ruler
pencil
rubber (just in case)
scissors
compass
sticky tape or glue
coloured pencils

1 Using a pencil and ruler, draw a grid of squares 2cm by 2cm over all your card.

2 PIECE A
FACE OF THE GAS MASK
On your grid, copy the gas mask face square for square. Remember to draw the mask window, and the fold lines. Cut it out. Cut the window out too. Crease along the fold lines. Colour the mask on the side without the grid. Fold the mask round so that flap A goes over flap B. Stick A to B.

3 PIECE B
GAS MASK STRAPS
Draw three straps. Each one should be 26cm long and 2cm wide. Cut them out. Stick them to the gas mask face at points C, D and E.

4 PIECE C
AIR FILTER
On your grid, copy the air filter square for square. Remember to draw the cut and fold lines. Cut it out. Cut along the short cut lines. Crease along the fold lines. Fold it round so that flap A goes under point B. Make sure the grid lines are on the inside of the tube. Stick A to B.

5 PIECE D
END OF AIR FILTER
With the compass draw a circle 8cm across. Inside the first circle draw another, 4.5cm across. Make a pattern of holes inside the inner circle. Cut around the edge of the large circle. Make short cuts from the outside edge to the edge of the inner circle. This will make lots of small flaps. Crease the flaps along the folds. Stick the filter end into the end of the air filter. Stick the air filter into the end of the gas mask face.

3 MAY 1943
Part-time war work made compulsory for women aged eighteen to forty-five.

17 MAY 1943
RAF bombers use 'bouncing' bombs to destroy dams in Germany.

23 MAY 1943
Massive RAF bombing raid on the German city of Dortmund.

30 JUNE 1943
Road signs taken down at the start of the war are put back.

Drawing up the pieces

PIECE D

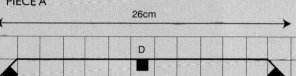

8cm diameter circle

1.5cm deep cuts

PIECE A

26cm

D

C

E

WINDOW

A FOLD

FOLD B

18cm

A FOLD

FOLD B

2cm PIECE B

26cm

B

CUTS

FOLD

A

17cm

6.5cm

PIECE C

A 'Mickey Mouse' gas mask.

WARNING!

If you find an old gas mask, don't try it on, no matter how tempted you are. Old gas masks contain dangerous chemicals and asbestos.

I think children in the 1940s thought it was fun to wear gas masks. Ben
I wouldn't have liked to wear one. Thomas

FACTBOX

About gas masks

Thirty-eight million gas masks were issued.

Poison gas was never used against Britain, so the gas masks were never needed.

Masks made from bright red rubber were issued to very young children. They were called 'Mickey Mouse' masks, and were meant to look fun to wear.

Babies were too small to wear gas masks. Instead, they had gas-proof containers which covered their whole bodies.

19 JULY 1943
Massive raid on the Italian capital, Rome, by USAAF bombers.

27 JULY 1943
Massive RAF bombing raid on the German city of Hamburg.

17 AUGUST 1943
RAF bombing raid on the German factory making V weapons.

4 OCTOBER 1943
Massive RAF bombing raid on the German city of Frankfurt.

What did you do in the war?

If you think the Second World War was a long time ago in the past, as Ben and Thomas did, then maybe you should stop and think again. The 1940s is a recent part of Britain's long history, so recent that there are many ways you can find out about it for yourself.

For lots of people alive in Britain today, the events of the war are fresh in their minds. These people were eyewitnesses to the events you've read about in this book and there's no better way of finding out about history than by talking to someone who was really there.

The Hymers meet an eyewitness.

Talking to an eyewitness

Who do we mean by an eyewitness? An eyewitness is someone who has personal memories of the war years. Here are some eyewitnesses you could talk to:

A man or woman who served in the armed services: the army, the navy or the air force.

A man or woman who served in the Home Guard – volunteers who kept watch over factories and railway stations, and who were on the look-out for spies and invaders.

A man or woman who served in the emergency services: fire, police or ambulance.

A man or woman who was an evacuee.

A woman who was in the 'Land Army'.

What did you do in the war?

Did you stay in Britain, or did you go abroad?
(Find out where they were.)

Did you wear a uniform?
(If the person did, then ask what it was like?)

What do you remember about rationing?

What did you do when you heard an air-raid siren?

When you have found an eyewitness, ask them if they would mind answering your questions. To the left are some questions you could ask.

Recording your information

Use a notebook to write down all the things your eyewitness tells you. If you have a cassette recorder, ask if it will be all right for you to tape the interview.

Service medals

The men and women who served in the armed forces were awarded medals such as these. You might find some in your search for 1940s evidence.

6 JUNE 1944
D-Day. Allied forces land in Normandy, France, beginning the invasion of Europe.

14 JUNE 1944
First German flying bomb, the VI 'doodle-bug', lands on Britain.

3 JULY 1944
Any children still in London are evacuated because of flying bombs.

31 JULY 1944
Germans retreat from Normandy, northern France.

Objects as evidence

Many people kept things from the war years. Some items were souvenirs, perhaps brought back by soldiers who served overseas, or kept by civilians who held on to items used in Britain. No matter what the objects are, they are evidence of the war, and of life in wartime Britain. You could ask members of your family, your friends' families and your neighbours if they have anything to show you from the 1940s. You will probably be surprised at what they might have, stored away in cupboards, attics and sheds. The photograph below and the list on the right show some items you might find.

MEDALS

GAS MASKS

PHOTOGRAPHS

IDENTIFICATION CARDS

RATION BOOKS

BADGES AND BUTTONS FROM UNIFORMS

INFORMATION LEAFLETS

NEWSPAPER CUTTINGS

FACTBOX

Other evidence

Use your library
Ask the librarian to show you the local collection. It contain books your area in the time. Find out what it was like then.

Wartime defences
There are many air-lters, pill-boxes fields dotted e country. if there are ar you. Again, ocal library might be able to help.

3 AUGUST 1944
Germans abandon the Channel Islands.

25 AUGUST 1944
Allies march into Paris. The German troops there surrender.

9 SEPTEMBER 1944
First German V2 rocket lands on London.

17 SEPTEMBER 1944
The blackout is partially lifted.

37

Women at war

The Second World War affected every person in Britain. For women, it was a time of great changes. Their lives would never be the same again. They played a vital role, doing the work of the men who were away fighting the war. They worked on the land and in factories, making parachutes, ammunition and many other things needed to support the army, air force and navy.

At home, housewives and mothers took over the roles of husbands and fathers. Without their valuable work in all aspects of wartime life British children like Ben and Thomas, would have suffered. As Ben and Thomas realised, women played a major role in 1940s Britain.

WOMEN OF BRITAIN
COME INTO THE FACTORIES
ASK AT ANY EMPLOYMENT EXCHANGE FOR ADVICE AND FULL DETAILS

Marguerite Patten

Marguerite Patten studied cookery before the Second World War. Her first job was as a junior home economist with an electricity company. In 1942, she became one of the Food Advisers to the Ministry of Food. It was her job to teach people how to cook with the limited ingredients then available. Her first cookery demonstration was to a group of people in the market square in Cambridge. Marguerite worked in East Anglia, showing people how to make their rations go further, and how to cook tasty and healthy meals from them. In 1942 she took over the Ministry of Food Bureau in Harrods, London, and helped British people and refugees from other countries too. She became one of the nation's favourite cooks.

Marguerite Patten has written 167 cookery books, she helped to launch frozen fish fingers in Britain after the war, and in 1991 she was awarded the OBE for 'services to the art of cookery'.

Barrage balloons were used as defence against enemy aircraft. Before the war, women such as these would not have been involved in such physical work.

11 NOVEMBER 1944
The 1,733,032 men and women of the Home Guard are released from duty.

20 NOVEMBER 1944
Streetlights are switched on again in London.

3 DECEMBER 1944
Home Guard disbanded.

6 DECEMBER 1944
Queen Elizabeth thanks the women of Britain for their war work.

WOMEN WORKERS
TRUE OR FALSE QUESTIONNAIRE

Read carefully each of the statements. Decide whether they are true or false and put a cross through the circle you think is correct.

1. Before the war, most women did not go out to work.
Ⓣ Ⓕ

2. Some women flew fighter planes.
Ⓣ Ⓕ

3. Women were allowed to fight in battle.
Ⓣ Ⓕ

4. 'Land Girls' were women who worked on farms.
Ⓣ Ⓕ

5. Mothers with babies were expected to do war work.
Ⓣ Ⓕ

6. After 1943, all women between the ages of eighteen and fifty were expected to work.
Ⓣ Ⓕ

7. Women served on board submarines
Ⓣ Ⓕ

8. Women did the work of men in factories.
Ⓣ Ⓕ

9. Women who gave homes to evacuees were called 'hosts'.
Ⓣ Ⓕ

10. Some women teachers were evacuated with their pupils.
Ⓣ Ⓕ

11. Air-raid patrol wardens were always men.
Ⓣ Ⓕ

12. The Women's Voluntary Service (WVS) helped people by providing refreshments, collecting metal for recycling, and making clothes and blankets.
Ⓣ Ⓕ

13. Women worked in branches of the army, navy and air force.
Ⓣ Ⓕ

14. Some women nurses went to work near battlefields.
Ⓣ Ⓕ

15. Women were paid the same as men for the same work.
Ⓣ Ⓕ

How well do you think you've done?
Turn to page 46 to check your answers.

Women's Land Army

Farm work was one of the most important jobs women did in the Second World War. The Woman's Land Army (WLA) was set up on 1 July 1939. By 1943 more than 100,000 women had gone to work on Britain's farms. They were known as 'Land Girls'. Throughout the war years these women ploughed fields, grew crops, gathered the harvests and tended to farm animals. Their work provided food for the nation.

Many women worked in munitions factories, making bombs and bullets for the armed forces.

Ben and Thomas's grandmother wearing her Women's Voluntary Service uniform.

10 DECEMBER 1944
The International Committee of the Red Cross is awarded the Nobel Prize for Peace.

27 JANUARY 1945
Russian troops capture the Auschwitz concentration camp in Poland.

14 FEBRUARY 1945
The city of Dresden, Germany, is destroyed by RAF and USAAF bombers.

EARLY MARCH 1945
Anne Frank dies in the Bergen-Belsen concentration camp.

Entertainment

Children's toys and games of the 1940s were much simpler than the ones children have today. Indoors, boys and girls enjoyed wooden jigsaws, card games and making models. They had dolls and toy soldiers too. Outside, they played football with balls made from sewn leather — much harder and heavier than today's footballs. And they had bikes, scooters and dolls' prams. Sometimes, events were organised for the whole community, as Ben and Thomas found out one night when they went to a Beetle drive.

Wartime wordsearch

Search for the wartime words hidden in the word square. They're hidden from left to right, right to left, and diagonally. Tick them off as you find them.

```
K B A A N C K R R C R
S L G S E E U C A V E
A A C K R C S R T C T
M C Z A I R R A I D L
S K Z Z S A E C O A E
A O Z T A C B A N G H
G U N A I K M C I Z S
N T N G K L O K N K R
D O O D L E B U G S Z
```

1 EVACUEES

2 RATIONING

3 AIR RAID

4 DOODLEBUGS

5 SHELTER

6 SIREN

7 GAS MASK

8 BOMBERS

9 BLACKOUT

10 BLITZ

Turn to page 46 to check your answers.

> I think the 1940s toys and games were better because they were good fun. Thomas

1 APRIL 1945
Plans made for evacuees to return to their homes.

15 APRIL 1945
Allied troops capture the concentration camp at Bergen-Belsen.

30 APRIL 1945
Allied troops march into Berlin, the German capital.

30 APRIL 1945
Adolf Hitler, the German leader, kills himself.

The Beetle game for two or more players

Beetle is best played with a lot of people – fast!

1 Each player needs a Beetle card, like the one below. All you need to do is draw up a grid of twelve boxes on a sheet of paper. Each box is for one game of Beetle.

2 Each player rolls a dice. The player with the highest number goes first, then the other players follow in a clockwise direction.

3 You must roll a 6 to begin.

4 When you have rolled a 6, you draw the Beetle's body in the first box on your grid.

5 Each time you roll a number, match it with the Beetle numbers to see which part of the Beetle you can draw next. If you roll a 3, you draw a leg; a 2 means a feeler, and so on.

6 You cannot draw the eyes or feelers until you have drawn the head.

7 The first person to draw a complete Beetle is the winner of the round. Twelve rounds make a complete game.

THE BEETLE GAME

1	2	3
4	5	6
7	8	9
10	11	12

BEETLE NUMBERS

Body........6
Head........5
Tail........4
6 x Legs........3 each
2 x Feelers........2 each
2 x Eyes........1 each

The toys and games we have today are more exciting than the ones in the 1940s. Ben

7 MAY 1945
Germany surrenders.

8 MAY 1945
VE Day (Victory in Europe). The war in Europe ends.

18 JUNE 1945
The end of military service for many members of the armed forces.

26 JUNE 1945
United Nations formed.

Old money

In Britain today we have a system of currency based on pounds and pence. It's called the decimal system and it is based on counting in tens. Before the decimal system we used a system based on counting in twelves. The old system used pounds, shillings and pence. There were 12 pennies in a shilling, and 20 shillings in a pound, which added up to 240 pennies in 1 pound (12 x 20 = 240).

Put yourself in the place of children from the 1940s, just as Ben and Thomas did. There were no calculators to help 1940s children with their arithmetic – they learned how to count in their heads and on their fingers. Have a go at these simple sums and read about Britain's old money on the opposite page.

How far will their money go today?

Can you count in old money?

Have a go at working out these simple sums. Use the information on the opposite page to help you. Remember, 1940s children didn't have calculators, so see if you can work out the answers by counting in your head and on your fingers.

Turn to page 47 to check your answers.

1. How many halfpennies (½d) make one threepence (3d)?

2. How many threepences (3d) make one sixpence (6d)?

3. How many sixpences (6d) make one half-crown (2s 6d)?

4. How many farthings (¼d) make one shilling (1s)?

5. How many threepences (3d) make one florin (2s)?

6. How many pennies (1d) make one sixpence (6d)?

7. How many pennies (1d) make one half-crown (2s 6d)?

8. How many pennies (1d) make one-shilling-and-seven-pence (1s 7d)?

9. How many halfpennies (½d) make eleven-pence-halfpenny (11½d)?

10. How many farthings (¼d) make one-shilling-and-four-pence-three-farthings (1s 4¾d)?

5 JULY 1945
Winston Churchill loses the general election.

12 JULY 1945
54,317 evacuees had returned to London.

31 JULY 1945
The blackout is completely lifted.

6 AUGUST 1945
The first atomic bomb is dropped, on Hiroshima, Japan.

Britain's old currency

These are the main coins used in Britain's old system of money. Each coin is shown its actual size. In addition, there was also a 5 shilling piece, which was called a crown (25p), but it was very rarely used. There were also banknotes – a 10 shilling note (50p), £1 and £5. The £1 note was coloured green, but in the Second World War a shortage of ink meant that some notes were printed in blue.

FARTHING (¼d)

Metal: Copper alloy

Diameter: 20mm

Number to the pound: 960

Number to the shilling: 48

Number to the penny: 4

HALFPENNY (½d)

Metal: Copper alloy

Diameter: 25mm

Number to the pound: 480

Number to the shilling: 24

Number to the penny: 2

PENNY (1d)

Metal: Copper alloy

Diameter: 30mm

Number to the pound: 240

Number to the shilling: 12

SILVER THREEPENCE (3d)

Nickname: 'Joey'

Metal: Silver alloy

Diameter: 15mm

Number to the pound: 80

Number to the shilling: 4

BRASS THREEPENCE (3d)

Metal: Brass alloy

Diameter: 21mm (12-sided)

Number to the pound: 80

Number to the shilling: 4

SIXPENCE (6d)

Nickname: 'Tanner'

Metal: Silver alloy (later, nickel)

Diameter: 20mm

Number to the pound: 40

Number to the shilling: 2

SHILLING (1s)

Nickname: 'Bob'

Metal: Silver alloy (later nickel)

Diameter: 24mm

Number to the pound: 20

FLORIN (2s)

Nickname: 'Two-bob bit'

Metal: Silver alloy (later nickel)

Diameter: 28mm

Number to the pound: 10

HALF-CROWN (2s 6d)

Nickname: 'Half a dollar' or 'Two and a kick'

Metal: Silver alloy (later nickel)

Diameter: 32mm

Number to the pound: 8

9 AUGUST 1945
Nagasaki, Japan, is destroyed by an atomic bomb.

14 AUGUST 1945
Japan surrenders.

15 AUGUST 1945
VJ Day (Victory in Japan). The war in the east ends.

8 JUNE 1946
The King sends a message to British children saying they should be proud of their country

Fabulous or frightful forties

How much do you know now about the 1940s? Have you decided if it was a fabulous time or a frightful time? Maybe you're still thinking about it.

Now that you've read through this book, you'll know a whole lot more about life in Britain in the 1940s, particularly about the six years of the Second World War. Test your new-found knowledge with this quiz – all the answers can be found somewhere in the book. Good luck!

FRIEND TO ALL
The war helped to make some people into celebrities – they became household names.

2: What was Marguerite Patten famous for?

a) Her wartime dancing

b) Her wartime singing

c) Her wartime cooking

SAFETY SHELTER
Families took cover in metal shelters in their gardens.

1: What was the name of the shelter?

a) Archerson shelter

b) Anderson shelter

c) Allenson shelter

LIGHTS OUT
At night, people sealed their windows and doors to stop light from escaping into the dark.

3: What was the time of darkness at night called?

a) The blackout

b) The darkout

c) The lightout

HOT WATER
People were asked to use less hot water in their homes.

4: How much water were people told they should bathe in?

a) Less than 4 inches (10cm)

b) Less than 5 inches (12½cm)

c) Less than 6 inches (15cm)

THEY HAD A NAME FOR IT
Some things have disappeared, such as rationing, old money, and Spitfires.

5: If you had a 'Tanner', what would you do with it?

a) Eat it

b) Spend it

c) Fly it

HEAVY BOMBER

Children quickly learned how to identify war planes, telling friend from foe.

6: Which country had a bomber plane called the Flying Fortress?

a) Britain

b) Germany

c) USA

FLYING BOMB

Germany's secret weapon, the V1, was fired at Britain in the closing months of the war.

8: Which of these nicknames was not used for the V1 flying bomb?

a) Doodlebug

b) Doodlebomb

c) Buzz-bomb

YOUR BEST FRIEND

The government used cartoon characters to explain information about food to children.

7: Which cartoon character was called the 'children's best friend'?

a) Doctor Carrot

b) Mickey Mouse

c) Potato Pete

NEVER NEEDED

The government issued all sorts of things to the public: some were useful, some were not.

9: What were people given which they never used?

a) Identification labels

b) Ration books

c) Gas masks

GROW YOUR OWN

People grew their own food, in their gardens and on allotments.

10: How many allotments were there in 1943?

a) 3.5 million

b) 35 million

c) 350 million

EVACUATION TIME

As war began, tens of thousands of children were evacuated to safe areas.

11: What was the name of the evacuation operation?

a) Operation Safe Areas

b) Operation Countryside

c) Operation Pied Piper

FORTIES FASHIONS

The shortage of textiles meant that some clothes were made from unusual materials.

12: What were offcuts of parachute nylon made into?

a) Underwear

b) Handkerchiefs

c) Dresses

How well do you think you've done? Turn to page 47 to check your answers. Will you be a wartime wizard or not?

Answers

PAGES 10–11
FORTIES FLASHBACK

1 c. George VI ☐
2 c. Winston Churchill ☐
3 b. 1939 to 1945 ☐
4 a. The Channel Islands ☐
5 c. London ☐
6 b. 240 ☐
7 b. Spam ☐
8 c. Jet plane ☐
9 c. Adolf Hitler ☐
10 a. Children's House ☐
YOUR SCORE ☐

PAGES 20–21
TELL-TALE TRACKS

A Person pushing
a wheelbarrow ☐
B Person with a wooden
leg and a walking stick ☐
C Person turning cartwheels ☐
D Person on stilts ☐
E Person with a hoop ☐
F Horse and cart ☐
G Tricycle ☐
YOUR SCORE

PAGE 27
I-SPY PLANES

1 = B Spitfire ☐
2 = D Hurricane ☐
3 = I Boeing B-17
Flying Fortress ☐
4 = F Heinkel 111 ☐
5 = E Flying bomb or V1 ☐
6 = H Junkers 88 ☐
7 = J Messerschmitt 109 ☐
8 = A Focke-Wulf 190 ☐
9 = G Lancaster ☐
10 = C Dornier 217 ☐
YOUR SCORE ☐

PAGE 39
WOMEN WORKERS – TRUE OR FALSE QUESTIONNAIRE

1 True ☐
2 True ☐
3 False ☐
4 True ☐
5 False ☐
6 True ☐
7 False ☐
8 True ☐
9 True ☐
10 True ☐
11 False ☐
12 True ☐
13 True ☐
14 True ☐
15 False ☐
YOUR SCORE ☐

PAGE 40 WORDSEARCH

```
K B A A N C K R R C R
S L G S E E U C A V E
A A C K R C S R T C T
M C Z A I R R A I D L
S K Z Z S A E C O A E
A O Z T A C B A N G H
G U N A I K M C I Z S
N T N G K L O K N K R
D O O D L E B U G S Z
```

YOUR SCORE (ONE FOR EACH WORD FOUND) ☐

PAGE 42
CAN YOU COUNT IN OLD MONEY?

1 6 halfpennies ☐
2 2 threepences ☐
3 5 sixpences ☐
4 48 farthings ☐
5 8 threepences ☐
6 6 pennies ☐
7 30 pennies ☐
8 19 pennies ☐
9 23 halfpennies ☐
10 67 farthings ☐

YOUR SCORE ☐

PAGES 44–45
FABULOUS OR FRIGHTFUL FORTIES?

1 b. Anderson shelter ☐
2 c. Her wartime cooking ☐
3 a. The blackout ☐
4 b. Less than 5 inches (12½cm) ☐
5 b. Spend it ☐
6 c. USA ☐
7 a. Doctor Carrot ☐
8 b. Doodlebomb ☐
9 c. Gas masks ☐
10 a. 3.5 million ☐
11 c. Operation Pied Piper ☐
12 a. Underwear ☐

YOUR SCORE ☐

ARE YOU A WARTIME WIZARD OR NOT?
Add all your scores together, then see how you rate:

0 to 20 sheep's-head stew and lumpy mash for you!

21 to 40 you deserve an extra sausage for tea!

41 to 60 award yourself a double ration of sweets!

61 to 74 break open and enjoy that big bar of chocolate you've saved from your rations!

Find out more

BOOKS: STORIES ABOUT LIFE IN THE SECOND WORLD WAR

Big Tom, by Jean Ure (Collins, 2000).
Set in wartime London, the story features a family who must come to terms with the sudden, dramatic changes the war brings

Blitz, by Robert Westall (Collins, 1995).
Four powerful stories exploring the effects of the war on the lives of young people.

Carrie's War, by Nina Bawden (Puffin, 2001).
A brother and sister are evacuated from London to Wales.

Goodnight Mr Tom, by Michelle Magorian (Longman, 2000).
An evacuee goes to stay with an elderly host in the country.

The Machine Gunners, by Robert Westall (Macmillan, 1994).
Classic adventure about a boy's wartime experience.

When the Siren Wailed, by Noel Streatfield (Collins, new edition 2000).
A story about wartime children evacuated to Dorset.

BOOKS: INFORMATION AND HISTORY TITLES

Horrible Histories: The Blitzed Brits, by Terry Deary (Scholastic, 1994).
Horrible Histories: The Woeful Second World War, by Terry Deary (Scholastic, 1999).
Serious wartime information, revealed in a light-hearted style.

History of Britain: The Blitz, by Andrew Langley (Hamlyn, 1995).
History of Britain: The Home Front, by Andrew Langley (Hamlyn, 1995).
The experiences of men, women and children in wartime Britain.

Wartime Cookbook: Food and Recipes from the Second World War, by Anne and Brian Moses (Wayland, 1995).
All you need to know about wartime food, with recipes to recreate wartime meals.

Britain at War: Air Raids, by Martin Parsons (Wayland, 1999).
Britain at War: Rationing, by Martin Parsons (Wayland, 1999).
Britain at War: Evacuation, by Martin Parsons (Wayland, 1999).
Britain at War: Women's War, by Martin Parsons (Wayland, 1999).
Informative, illustrated accounts on specific wartime subjects.

PLACES TO VISIT

Britain at War Experience, 64 Tooley Street, London SE1 2TF (020 7403 3171).
Hands-on museum, where you can try on helmets, gas masks and uniforms.

Cabinet War Rooms, King Charles Street, London SW1A 2AQ (020 7416 5320).
The British government's secret wartime headquarters.

Eden Camp, Malton, North Yorkshire YO17 6RT (01653 697777).
Extensive display of wartime British life, housed in prisoner-of-war huts built in 1942.

HMS Belfast, Morgan's Lane, Tooley Street, London SE1 2JH (020 7940 6300).
Europe's last big-gun Second World War warship, moored on the River Thames.

Imperial War Museum, Lambeth Road, London SE1 6HZ (020 7416 5320).
Britain's national museum presenting the history of the nation's wars, including (from December 2000) an exhibition in which the 1940s house that the Hymers lived in is recreated.

Imperial War Museum, Duxford, Cambridgeshire CB2 4QR (01223 835000).
Britain's largest collection of aircraft, with many from the Second World War.

WEBSITES

www.channel4.com/1940house
Learn more about the 1940s house here.

www.normandy.eb.com
D-Day site with video clips, sound recordings and photos.

www.bbc.co.uk/education/lzone/soundbox/trans14.htm
Hear air raid sirens, bombs and famous wartime radio broadcasts.

www.battleofbritain.net
Information on the Battle of Britain.

www.westallswar.org.uk
Inspired by the books of Robert Westall, the site explores north-east England in the Second World War

www.thehistorynet.com
Huge site for history, with large Second World War section.

british-forces.com
History of the British armed forces, with much on the Second World War and wartime Britain.

www.iwm.org.uk
The Imperial War Museum's own site.